W9-ATO-871

MAY 1978
RECEIVED
OHIO DOMINICAN
COLLEGE LIBRARY
COLUMBUS, OHIO
43219

OHIO DOMINICAN COLLEGE LIBRARY
COLUMBUS, OHIO 43219

RUBENS

Published by Oxford University Press

RUBENS

A Biography by
ELIZABETH RIPLEY

With Drawings and
Paintings by Rubens

New York   HENRY Z. WALCK, INC., DISTRIBUTORS   1957

J
927.5
R

© OXFORD UNIVERSITY PRESS, INC., 1957
LIBRARY OF CONGRESS CATALOG CARD NUMBER: 57-11450
PRINTED IN THE UNITED STATES OF AMERICA

ILLUSTRATIONS

104606

ONE DAY in 1590, Peter Paul Rubens set out on horseback toward a castle outside of Antwerp. The year before his older brother, Philip, had left home to become secretary to the Mayor of Brussels. Now fourteen-year-old Peter Paul was to serve as a page to a Flemish countess.

The countess was charmed by the gracious manners of her tall handsome page, who spoke four languages and could recite pages of Latin poetry. Although the boy's father had died when his son was very young, Peter Paul's mother had managed to send him to a good school, where the eager boy learned quickly.

Peter Paul spent many hours waiting on the countess, but he sometimes found time to hunt on the countess' fine horses. His happiest hours were spent reading and copying pictures from the beautiful books in the castle library. He wrote his mother that he wished to become a painter, and persuaded her to allow him to return to Antwerp to study art.

From his first teacher Rubens learned the craft of painting and drawing. His next teacher taught him to love the art of ancient Rome, and urged his talented pupil to visit Italy.

Sadly twenty-three-year-old Rubens said good-by to his mother who was far from well. For five weeks he rode over snowy mountains until he reached the brilliant city of Venice. The rich coloring of the Venetian paintings dazzled him and he began at once to copy many of them.

In Venice Rubens met the erratic Duke of Mantua, who invited him to become his court painter. Soon after Rubens arrived in Mantua the Duke invited him to accompany him to Florence, where beautiful Marie de'Medici was to be married to the King of France. Rubens noted every detail of the magnificent ceremony—the princess' jeweled gown, her small lap dog, and the glittering array of royal guests.

Rubens noted other things in Florence, too. He admired the works of the Italian painters who had lived one hundred years before. He copied a tumultuous battle scene by the great Leonardo da Vinci. Today Rubens' drawing is all that remains of Leonardo's famous picture.

RUBENS' DRAWING AFTER LEONARDO DA VINCI'S
BATTLE OF ANGHIARI

Louvre, Paris

Photo Giraudon

At the court of Mantua, Rubens made copies of the paintings in the Duke's collection, and the Duke gave the copies to princes from whom he wished to borrow money. In his spare time Rubens loved to listen to the conversations of the distinguished scholars who visited the court. Sometimes he took long rides on the Duke's magnificent horses. He sketched the horses, too, and the lions, tigers and camels in the Duke's menagerie.

One day the adventuresome Duke of Mantua suddenly decided to lead his small army against the Turks who threatened to invade Italy. The Duke did not ask Rubens to accompany him on his wild campaign. Instead, he gave his court painter permission to visit Rome. Rubens was delighted, for he longed to see the works of art he had learned so much about in Antwerp.

The paintings by Michelangelo on the ceiling of the Pope's chapel impressed him deeply, and he copied some of the great artist's powerful figures. He sketched stately buildings and antique statues. Then one day his brother, Philip, wrote him from Brussels that Archduke Albert, who governed Flanders at that time, had heard of Rubens' talent and commissioned him to paint a picture of Saint Helena discovering the true cross on which Jesus died. The Archduke planned to give the picture to a new church in Rome.

This was Rubens' first big religious painting, and in it he tried to show what he had learned in Italy. Against a rich Venetian background of ornate pillars, he painted the stiffly posed figure of Saint Helena, draped in an elaborate brocaded cloak, gazing devoutly toward heaven.

After two months of hard work Rubens' painting was finished, and the Duke of Mantua, who had returned defeated from his mad campaign, summoned his court painter to Mantua. Sadly Rubens prepared to leave the city where he still had so much to learn. But before he left Rome, a letter came from Philip, saying that he was coming to Italy on business. He planned to stop in Verona, a town not far from Mantua. Joyously Peter Paul packed his belongings and rode full speed in the direction of Verona.

ST. HELENA DISCOVERING THE TRUE CROSS:
SANTA CROCE ALTARPIECE

Chapel of Municipal Hospital, Grasse

The meeting of the Rubens brothers in Verona was a happy one. Peter Paul listened eagerly while Philip told him news of Antwerp. Their mother was not well, but she was happy about her youngest son's success in Italy. Antwerp was becoming a prosperous city. Although Flanders was still ruled by Spain, the people were content under the wise government of the Spanish Archduke Albert and his good wife, Isabella.

Peter Paul was delighted when his brother introduced him to a learned scholar from Antwerp who had been Philip's teacher. The professor invited Peter Paul, Philip and another of his pupils to gather around a table and discuss philosophy. Peter Paul never forgot that interesting meeting. Nine years later he painted a picture of the professor and his pupils.

The lean, dark-bearded professor, handsomely dressed in a coat with a wide fur collar, sat between his two pupils. His finger pointed to a passage in the book in front of him. To his right was Philip, holding a pen in his hand. Peter Paul stood humbly in the background. The velvet curtain behind his head was pulled aside to show an Italian landscape. Because the other pupil had just written a book about Seneca, Rubens placed a bust of the Greek philosopher in a niche above the scholar's head.

But Rubens could not linger in Verona. Impatiently the Duke of Mantua waited his return, for he was making plans to send his gracious court painter to the court of Spain.

THE FOUR PHILOSOPHERS

Pitti Gallery, Florence

Photo Alinari

In the spring of 1603, the Duke of Mantua wrote to his ambassador in Spain that he was sending "Peter Paul the Fleming" bearing gifts for the Spanish King.

As soon as Rubens returned from Verona, he started to make preparations for his journey. He gave careful instructions about the packing of rare paintings, sparkling crystals and brightly polished guns, and about the care of the seven spirited horses which were also presents for the King. Early in May Rubens and his train of horses and carriages set off over mountainous roads toward the harbor where a ship waited to take them to Spain. Terrible storms rocked the ship carrying Rubens' precious cargo. When the crates were unloaded on the shore of Spain, torrential rains poured down upon them. Rubens and his caravan struggled along muddy roads until they arrived at the Spanish court. But King Philip was away, and Rubens was told he must wait until His Majesty returned.

Rubens set to work unpacking the Duke's paintings, but when he opened the rain-soaked crates he found that the glowing canvases had rotted. Brusquely the Duke of Mantua's ambassador ordered him to make copies of the paintings before the King's return. Rubens set to work immediately, and in just two months the copies had been completed.

On a sunny July day the King and Queen received Rubens in the royal gardens. Graciously the Flemish painter presented the guns, the crystals and the sleek horses. When he held up the freshly painted canvases, King Philip never suspected that they were copies.

One member of the court was especially impressed by the talented Flemish painter. This was the King's prime minister, the Duke of Lerma. He asked Rubens to paint his portrait. Rubens sketched the Duke astride a prancing horse. Daringly he showed the horse head-on, instead of from the side as other artists had done. When the portrait was finished, the Duke of Lerma was so pleased that he offered Rubens more commissions.

For one whole year Rubens painted pictures for the court of Spain, but he was homesick for Italy. At last the Duke of Mantua ordered Rubens to return.

THE DUKE OF LERMA

Louvre, Paris

Photo Giraudon

As soon as Rubens returned from Spain, the Duke asked him to paint three pictures to decorate the altar wall of his favorite church in Mantua. The central panel would show the Duke and his family worshipping the Holy Trinity. The impetuous Duke, who longed to be liked, hoped in this way to show that he had a pious and generous nature.

Rubens set to work immediately. He painted a picture of the Holy Trinity surrounded by angels. Below was the kneeling figure of the handsome Duke dressed in ermine, looking devoutly toward heaven. Beside him knelt his hunch-backed father, and facing the Duke, his wife, and his mother dressed as a nun. Rubens remembered the glowing paintings he had seen in Venice, and he painted the richly costumed figures in brilliant tones of reds and golds against a landscape framed by ornate twisted pillars. The Duke was so pleased that Rubens had shown him in a pose of deep devotion that he paid his painter well.

Although the Duke was delighted with the picture, Rubens knew that he still had much to learn. He longed to return to Rome in order to continue his studies. Philip wrote him that he had been made librarian to a cardinal in Rome, and that he was living comfortably in a house with two servants. He urged his brother to visit him.

Rubens waited many weeks before the Duke gave him permission to leave Mantua, but at last one day, Rubens set out happily to join his brother in Rome.

TRINITY ADORED BY GONZAGA FAMILY

Mantua Academy, Mantua

Rubens was overjoyed to be once more in Rome. With Philip he walked through the streets of the city, visiting shops where he picked out pieces of antique marble to start a collection. He loved to discuss the history of these rare pieces with the learned students who gathered at Philip's home. Sometimes he would sit until late in the evening talking about philosophy with the scholars who called on the Rubens brothers.

Peter Paul worked hard during the winter of 1607, because the Duke of Mantua had commissioned him to paint an altarpiece, which he planned to give to a new church in Rome. In two months Rubens painted a brilliant picture of "The Virgin Adored by Saints," but when it was hung above the altar of the new church, it looked like a blur of silvery tones. The Duke ordered the Fleming to remove the picture and paint another to replace it. Patiently Rubens set to work, but this time he painted the picture in the church, tilting the panel forward to receive the proper light.

Then one day news came from Antwerp that his mother was very ill. Philip left Rome immediately, but Peter Paul could not go with him, for he was still working on the painting for the Duke.

When the painting was finished he wrote modestly to the Duke's secretary, "If I am not mistaken, it is the least unsuccessful by my hand."

One October day in 1609 Rubens wrote the Duke that he would have to return to Antwerp because his mother was very ill. He packed his books, his pieces of marble and the first painting of "The Virgin Adored by Saints" which the church had returned to him. That same day he left Rome for the last time.

For two bitterly cold months Rubens rode over snowy mountains until at last he reached his home. But he arrived too late to see his mother again. With Philip he visited the church where his mother was buried. Some days later he returned to the church and hung the bright picture of "The Virgin Adored by Saints" above the spot where Maria Rubens lay.

THE VIRGIN ADORED BY SAINTS

Grenoble Museum, Grenoble

Rubens was thirty years old when he returned to Flanders. In eight years he had become a gracious ambassador, a distinguished scholar and an outstanding painter. Archduke Albert and his wife, Isabella, invited him to Brussels and asked him to become their court painter. They gave him a large salary and a gleaming gold chain to wear around his neck.

Philip and Peter Paul lived in their old home in Antwerp, until one day Philip told his brother that he was planning to marry. Peter Paul was delighted, for he knew the girl Philip had chosen.

"I myself will not dare to follow him," wrote Peter Paul to a friend in Rome, "for he has made such a choice that it seems inimitable."

Philip and his bride settled in Antwerp, and Peter Paul visited the couple often. It was there that he met lovely Isabella Brandt, seventeen-year-old daughter of a well-known lawyer. Isabella told him shyly that she admired his fine paintings. Rubens was charmed by her gentle manner.

Rubens called many times at the Brandt home, and soon he decided to ask Isabella's father for his daughter's hand. This was a happy day for Isabella, who like Rubens had fallen deeply in love.

Rubens and Isabella were married one October day in 1609. The handsome groom was dressed in white, his wavy blond hair brushed back from his face, beard trim and mustaches neatly twisted. Exquisite Isabella in a jeweled white satin gown looked radiant.

For one year the happy couple lived in the Brandt home. That same year Rubens painted a picture of himself seated with Isabella under a bower of honeysuckle. Rubens wore a wide black hat and a black and gold suit with a broad lace collar. Isabella sat on the ground beside him. Her delicate face was framed by a huge ruff and on her head was a tall yellow hat. Her quilted jacket was black and her skirt a rich crimson. Tenderly she rested her hand on that of her adored husband.

RUBENS AND ISABELLA BRANDT

Alte Pinakothek, Munich

Early each morning Rubens arrived at his studio where young artists were busily working on his partly painted canvases, for Rubens needed help in filling the many commissions which came to him. He would move from one canvas to another, instructing one artist how to paint the fine detail on a lace ruff in a portrait of the Archduke Albert, or complimenting another on the beautifully painted bunch of grapes held by a little child.

He would stop in front of a huge canvas on which was sketched a picture of the Virgin and Child adored by the Three Kings. Beside the easel stood Rubens' small sketch of the scene painted in bold colors. Rubens would pick up a brush and show an assistant how to fill in some of the figures which had been outlined on the large canvas, and instruct another about the painting of the marble pillars and dark sky in the background.

When the painting of "The Adoration of the Kings" was finished, it was hung in Antwerp's Town Hall. The city governors who had ordered it were so proud of the great work by their Flemish artist that they decided to give it as a present to the ambassador from Spain.

More and more orders for religious paintings poured into the Rubens workshop. Bishops and cardinals wanted Rubens' glowing canvases to decorate their churches. He was asked to paint an altarpiece showing the raising of the cross for one of Antwerp's largest churches. Remembering the disappointment of the poorly lighted altarpiece in Rome, Rubens set up his canvas in the church and started to paint.

Slashing sideways across the panel, Rubens placed the cross to which was nailed the body of Jesus. A group of men, stripped to the waist, were straining every muscle to place the cross upright. In the right panel, soldiers on horseback directed the raising of the cross, while on the left, terrified children and grief-stricken men and women watched the agonizing scene.

Rubens painted a dramatic picture which everyone could understand. The brilliantly lighted figures stood out strikingly against a stormy background. Forcefully they told of the intense tragedy of that moment.

ERECTION OF THE CROSS
(Central panel)

Antwerp Cathedral, Antwerp

Copyright A.C.L. Brussels

Rubens was now the most famous painter in Flanders. Art students flocked to his studio hoping to study with the great master and many had to be turned away.

Rubens worked from sunrise to sunset. He got up every morning at four o'clock, went to church and was back at his studio ready to paint as soon as daylight began to filter through the window. At sunset he took a brief gallop out into the country, stopping on his way home to give directions about the building of his new house which he had designed. After a quiet supper with Isabella, he would talk about art, philosophy and the latest books with the learned friends who gathered at his home.

In the spring of 1611 delicate, fair-haired Clara-Serena Rubens was born. Isabella was a tender and loving mother. Over and over Rubens painted his wife's gentle, radiant face in his pictures of the Mother Mary and the baby Jesus. Peter Paul was an adoring father. After a busy day at the workshop he loved to spend quiet hours with his wife and baby.

One evening Rubens told Isabella that he had signed an important contract with a company of archers who had asked him to paint a huge altarpiece for Antwerp's big cathedral. For three years Rubens worked on his painting of "The Descent from the Cross." When the picture was finished, the archers paid him well and presented Isabella with a beautiful pair of gloves.

One July day in 1614 the painting was solemnly dedicated in the great cathedral. Isabella, wearing the fine gloves which the archers had given her, stood beside her handsome husband. When she gazed at the picture which hung above the altar, she knew that Peter Paul had painted a masterpiece.

The picture showed a group of men tenderly lowering the body of Jesus from the cross, while three beautiful women reached up to receive it. Rubens had not tried to paint the scene in the smooth, formal manner of the Italians. In his own vigorous language he told a tale of noble suffering, and these stalwart, fair-haired men and radiant-skinned blond women were men and women of Flanders, intent on performing a tragic task.

THE DESCENT FROM THE CROSS

Antwerp Cathedral, Antwerp

Copyright A.C.L. Brussels

Just outside the busy streets of Antwerp, workmen were building Rubens' new home. Every afternoon Rubens clattered into the paved courtyard on his spirited, dapple-gray horse. Spreading out his beautifully drawn plans, he would give directions to his workmen.

Three arches linked his home with his workshop. Detailed drawings showed ornate pillars, urns and statues which decorated the buildings. There were two studios in the workshop—one for himself and another for his assistants—and rooms for his collection of paintings, rare books and priceless pieces of marble. He had plans for a garden, too, with a little pool sunk in a shady grotto.

Five years went by before the new house was ready, but it was in Rubens' magnificent mansion that Albert Rubens was born. Graciously Archduke Albert, kind ruler of Flanders, consented to become the boy's godfather.

On warm summer days Albert played in the shady garden and watched fascinated as strutting peacocks spread their brilliant tails. Sometimes he walked with his father to the big stables and fed carrots to the horses. On dark winter afternoons he and Clara-Serena sat before a crackling fire, and listened spellbound to the stories which Isabella read to them from a big book.

Albert was delighted when his father told him one day that he was bringing a real lion to live in the workshop. A German prince, Rubens explained, had commissioned him to paint a picture of a lion hunt. He planned to keep the lion for several weeks, so that he could sketch him many times.

Rubens' painting of "The Lion Hunt" was an exciting tangle of angry huntsmen, rearing horses and ferocious lions. Skilled Frans Snyders, one of Rubens' most talented assistants, painted several of the raging beasts. But some of the most beautiful drawings of animals that have ever been made are Rubens' sketches of majestic lions at rest.

RECUMBENT LION

The British Museum, London

Orders for Rubens' spirited hunting scenes poured into the workshop. He painted a picture of hunters on horseback, chasing wild boar through a beautiful wooded landscape. He painted another picture of turbaned Moors spearing a clumsy hippopotamus which sprawled on the back of a fierce, gaping crocodile.

For a Spanish general he painted an exciting wolf and fox hunt. It was a furious scene of wolves and foxes being attacked by dogs and huntsmen armed with spears. Teeth bared, the angry wolves defended themselves against the attack, while small foxes were being trampled underfoot. On the right was a handsome huntsman on a dapple-gray horse, who is supposed to be Rubens. He wore a green jacket and yellow boots. With sword drawn he prepared to attack the furious beasts below him. Lovely Isabella, elegantly dressed in red velvet, holding a falcon, rode beside him.

Lord Carleton, English ambassador to Holland, offered Rubens a costly chain of diamonds belonging to Lord Carleton's wife, in exchange for one of Rubens' "Lion Hunts." So pleased was the lord with the picture that he offered to exchange his fine collection of antique marble statues for more paintings by the Flemish artist.

In a letter to Lord Carleton, Rubens listed the pictures he was sending to England, describing each canvas in detail and taking care to mention those which were painted by his hand and the ones painted by assistants.

"I believe Your Excellency will be completely satisfied with them," Rubens wrote. "In short, in exchange for marbles to furnish one room, Your Excellency receives pictures to adorn an entire palace."

THE WOLF AND FOX HUNT

Metropolitan Museum of Art, New York City

When Albert Rubens was four years old his younger brother was born. His father named him Nicholas for an Italian nobleman he had met in Genoa. This same nobleman commisioned Rubens to pain an altarpiece for a church in Genoa. It was a big picture showing the Spanish saint Ignatius healing the insane. That same year Rubens told the story again in an altarpiece for a church in Antwerp.

Austere Saint Ignatius, dressed in white and gold, stood before the altar of a sumptuous church, hand outstretched toward the mad people below him. A brilliant light shone on the tortured group of sick people on the left; while on the right, a quiet group of mothers and children waited to receive the saint's blessing. Floating under the arched ceiling in the background were the evil spirits which the saint had cast out.

Every day orders for religious paintings came to Rubens' workshop. He painted two enormous pictures of the last judgment, filled with magnificently painted, nude figures cascading into hell. As each huge canvas was finished Rubens began another, always striving to make it better than the one before.

Then one day Rubens informed the Archduchesse Isabella that he would have to make a trip to Paris, for Marie de' Medici, widow of King Henry IV of France, had commissioned him to paint pictures of her life for the walls of her new palace. The Archduchesse was delighted that her gracious court painter was planning to visit the French court. Since Archduke Albert's death, one year before, the Archduchesse had often called on Rubens for advice in governing her country. Now, she believed, he would be able to help her make friends with the powerful rulers of France. So one day in 1621, Rubens set off for Paris, taking with him a tiny lap dog with a beautiful enamel collar, a present from the Archduchesse Isabella to Queen Marie de' Medici of France.

MIRACLES OF SAINT IGNATIUS LOYOLA

Kunsthistorisches Museum, Vienna

Marie de'Medici received Rubens in her palace. Bowing low, Rubens told the Queen that she looked even more beautiful than she had that day in Florence, twenty years before, when he had been a guest at her brilliant wedding.

The Queen was charmed by the gracious and good-looking artist. She invited him to walk through the rooms he was to decorate. In one gallery would be pictures of the life of her husband, Henry IV, who had died ten years before; and the walls of the next room would be decorated with paintings of the Queen's life. Marie de' Medici was delighted when Rubens described in detail the scenes he would illustrate and she urged him to sign a contract immediately.

Rubens agreed to paint twenty-one enormous pictures within four years. With confidence he faced the staggering task. "My talent is such," he wrote, "that no undertaking however vast in size or diversified in subject, has ever surpassed my courage."

A few weeks later Rubens returned to Antwerp. Albert and Nicholas ran to meet him when he galloped into the courtyard of his home, but little Clara-Serena could not move from her chair. Sadly Isabella told her husband that their little daughter had been ill and could no longer walk.

Early the next morning Rubens was hard at work painting sketches of the French Queen's life. He did not show the events exactly as they happened, for in every scene he painted figures of gods and goddesses, nymphs and cupids, which helped to tell the story of the picture.

In one painting gallant Henry IV, dressed in shining armor, admired the portrait of his future bride. A helmeted goddess, representing France, stood behind him urging him to marry the beautiful Italian princess. Two pretty cupids were carrying away the King's shield and helmet, which were no longer needed because Henry's marriage would bring peace between Italy and France. On a cloud above the King sat Jupiter and his wife, Juno, who represented Henry and his bride.

HENRY IV RECEIVES PORTRAIT OF
MARIE DE'MEDICI

Louvre, Paris

Every day Clara-Serena grew weaker, and in the spring of 1623 the little girl died. These were sad days for Isabella and Peter Paul.

That same year strong healthy Philip Rubens suddenly fell ill. Antwerp's best doctors could not save him. In a few days Peter Paul's beloved brother was dead.

Rubens planned a funeral worthy of his distinguished brother. When the long orations were over, Peter Paul hung a portrait he had painted of handsome Philip over his brother's impressive tomb. With a heavy heart he returned to his studio to work on his pictures for the French Queen.

In the spring of 1624, nine of the paintings were finished. Rubens carefully rolled up the sparkling canvases and set off for Paris in order to show them to the Queen.

So delighted was Marie de'Medici with the brilliant pictures, that she asked Rubens to finish the others before the marriage of her daughter to King Charles of England. In just one year Rubens would have to paint twelve enormous pictures. He set up a studio in the Queen's palace and hired skilled assistants.

Marie de'Medici visited the workshop often. She was delighted with the painting of her wedding and marvelled that Rubens had remembered every detail of her jeweled gown. She admired the glittering picture of her arrival in France. The newly married Queen, arrayed in shimmering white satin, stepped from a gold ship onto a sloping ramp. A helmeted goddess, France, greeted her with outstretched arms. Blond goddesses and long-haired gods of the sea held the boat in place while bearded Neptune directed the proceedings. In the sky floated a winged goddess trumpeting the Queen's arrival.

Work in the palace studio continued after Rubens returned to Antwerp. Through the fall and winter he wrote long letters giving directions to his assistants in Paris.

When spring came, twenty-one paintings had been finished and Rubens set off once more for France.

DEBARKATION OF MARIE DE'MEDICI
AT MARSEILLES

Louvre, Paris

On the day that the French princess, Henrietta Maria, was married to King Charles I of England, a throng of distinguished guests filed through the great hall which Rubens had decorated. Young King Louis, Marie de'Medici's son, stood for a long time in front of the biggest canvas, a regal picture of his mother's coronation. The majestic Queen, arrayed in a blue cloak lined with ermine, knelt at the altar, while a cardinal placed a crown upon her head. On her right was Prince Louis, holding aside his mother's cloak, while on the Queen's left stood her daughter, Princess Henrietta Maria. Henry IV watched the ceremony from a balcony. Two goddesses floated above the resplendent guests; one bearing a crown of peace, and the other showering golden coins upon the Queen.

The wedding of Marie de'Medici's daughter to the King of England was a brilliant one. Rubens took part in the festivities which lasted several days. He was introduced to the dashing Duke of Buckingham, prime minister to the English King. The Duke was charmed by the talented Flemish painter. He inquired with interest about Rubens' collection of antique marbles, and Rubens asked the Duke questions about affairs of state in England. Rubens stayed several weeks in Paris, planning pictures of the life of Henry IV and painting portraits of the royal family. He welcomed visitors to his studio and encouraged them to talk while he was painting. When conversation turned to politics, he listened carefully, so that he could report what he heard to the Archduchesse.

As soon as Rubens returned to Flanders he called on the Archduchesse to tell her the news of the French court. Buckingham was trying to make a treaty with France, Rubens reported, because he wanted to plunge his country into a war against Spain. The Archduchesse begged Rubens to help her to bring peace between Spain and England. Rubens assured her that he was ready to serve the cause of peace.

"Now is the time to offer every service to the general welfare," he wrote to a friend.

CORONATION OF MARIE DE'MEDICI

Louvre, Paris

When Rubens returned to his home, Isabella greeted her husband affectionately. She looked pale and tired Rubens thought, but smilingly she assured her husband that she felt well. Albert and Nicholas listened eagerly while Rubens told them about the wedding of the princess.

Many pictures had been painted in his workshop while Rubens had been in Paris. He complimented able Frans Snyders, who had directed the work and congratulated one handsome young artist on his painting of a Madonna and Child. This sensitive young man had great talent, Rubens thought. Someday, he believed, Anthony Van Dyke would become a famous painter.

Twelve great pictures of "The Adoration of the Kings" had been finished in the workshop at the time Rubens was painting pictures for the Queen. Some of them were finished by assistants, but others Rubens painted with his own hand.

In thirteen days he painted a beautiful "Adoration" for the church where his mother and brother were buried. In the center of the canvas stood the fierce dark figure of the Moorish King, dressed in brilliant green. Feet spread, hands on hips, he gazed with amazement at the Christ Child. On the left stood a white-bearded King in a brocaded cloak of brilliant red. The handsome young King with blond wavy hair and beard who knelt before the Child wore a cloak of white and gold.

Shepherds, helmeted soldiers and the Kings' richly dressed attendants crowded into the stable to look with wonder at the radiant child. Two men on camels were bending forward under the arched doorway in order to gaze at the infant Jesus.

On the right, apart from the crowd stood the Mother Mary holding her child. A bright light illumined her lovely face, which was the face of Rubens' gentle wife, Isabella.

ADORATION OF THE MAGI

Antwerp Museum, Antwerp

Rubens was proud of his two good-looking, healthy sons. When they were babies he had painted their rosy-cheeked faces in his pictures of cherubs, and when they grew older his sturdy blond boys had appeared in some of his religious paintings. Then one day when Albert was eleven and Nicholas six, Rubens decided to paint their portrait. Isabella was delighted and told the boys to dress in their best clothes.

Albert felt very important, posing in his black velvet jacket slit with white, and wearing a broad-brimmed, black hat. He stood, one leg crossed in front of the other. A beautiful fur-lined glove dangled from the hand which rested protectingly on his younger brother's shoulder. In the other hand he held a book, because he was proud of the fine education his father was able to give him.

Nicholas wore a blue satin jacket slit with gold. Fancy red satin bows decorated his knees and his shoes. Feet planted firmly on the ground, he held in his hands a bird's perch to which a string was attached. Frowning slightly he fixed his eyes on the little bird which fluttered helplessly at the other end of the string.

Sometimes Isabella took her sewing to the studio and sat quietly while Rubens painted her sons' portrait. As each sure swift stroke of Rubens' brush brought the figures to life, she marvelled at her husband's skill.

In a few days the charming portrait was finished, and Rubens set to work once more on the many commissions which had come to him.

ALBERT AND NICHOLAS RUBENS

Lichtenstein Collection, Lichtenstein

One day the Archduchesse called Rubens to her palace to discuss a series of pictures she wanted him to paint. The pictures would be used for tapestry designs, she explained, and she planned to give the tapestries to a convent in Spain. The Archduchesse, who was a sincerely religious woman, chose as her subject, "The Triumph of Christian Religion." It was a difficult subject, but almost immediately Rubens was able to describe the pictures he would paint.

One picture called "The Defender of the Faith" would show saints, Popes and princes, and the Archduchesse wearing the robes of a nun, for, since her husband's death, she had dressed in convent robes.

Another picture called "The Triumph of Christian Worship Over Idolatry" would show a white-robed pagan priest, heathen worshippers and a cow which was about to be sacrificed, falling in confusion before a radiant angel who descended from heaven.

Rubens painted fifteen sketches telling the story of "The Triumph of Christianity." From the sketches, pictures were painted in the Rubens workshop; later, the paintings were copied for tapestries.

At the same time that Rubens was working on the tapestry designs, he was filling orders for Kings and princes in many countries in Europe. King Philip IV of Spain, son of the King that Rubens had met twenty years before, asked the Flemish artist to paint decorations for his hunting lodge. English lords and ladies wanted to have their portraits painted, and there were many orders for altarpieces.

Rubens was never too busy to spend a few hours each day with his family. He was anxious about Isabella, who looked pale and thin. She never complained, but one morning she was unable to move from her bed. Each day she grew weaker, and Antwerp's best doctors could not help her. In June, 1626, Isabella Rubens died.

This was a staggering blow for Peter Paul. "This loss strikes me to the core," he wrote to a friend. "It will be very difficult for me to separate my grief from the memory I shall cherish all my life of that person so dear and respected above all others."

THE TRIUMPH OF CHRISTIAN WORSHIP
OVER IDOLATRY

Prado, Madrid

During the long summer days Rubens worked in his studio and tried to forget his great sorrow, but in the evening his magnificent home seemed unbearably lonely. In every room were reminders of gentle Isabella.

"I should think a journey would be advisable," Rubens wrote to a friend, "to take me away from the many things which necessarily renew my sorrow." So, in the fall of 1626, Rubens wrote to the Duke of Buckingham's secretary in Paris that he was coming to discuss his collection of antique marbles which the Duke wanted to buy. But this was not the chief reason for Rubens' trip to Paris. The Archduchesse had asked Rubens to be her special ambassador to France in order to persuade Buckingham to make peace between Spain and England.

The Duke welcomed Rubens cordially and agreed to pay the price Rubens asked for his precious antique marbles. He commissioned Rubens to paint his portrait. While Rubens sketched Buckingham's proud, handsome face, the Duke talked about politics in Europe. So determined was the reckless and ambitious Duke to plunge his country into war, that Rubens was unable to persuade him to talk peace with Spain.

This was the discouraging news which Rubens reported to the Archduchesse. He assured her that he would continue to work for peace, and begged her to allow him to talk with the Duke of Buckingham's representative in Holland.

But Rubens' mission to Holland was not successful. When he returned to Flanders, the Archduchesse informed him that the King of Spain, fearing the warlike Buckingham, had made a secret treaty with France and was planning to invade England. This was shattering news for Rubens.

"I beg you to believe that I am doing all I can," he wrote to a friend, "but," he added, "the Gods willed otherwise."

DUKE OF BUCKINGHAM

Albertina, Vienna

"The Marquis is, I think, a prudent, active and diligent man," wrote Rubens about the Spanish general Spinola, King Philip's representative in Flanders.

Dressed in a tunic of gleaming armor the Marquis posed, while Rubens painted his portrait.

"(he) speaks little and is very reserved," Rubens wrote, "hearing everything and thinking none the less."

Like Rubens, Spinola hoped that war in Europe could be prevented and he urged the Spanish King to make peace with England. But the King sent word that he was not ready to make a peace treaty with England, until he had talked to Rubens about his conversations with Buckingham in Paris. So in the spring of 1628 the Archduchesse asked Rubens to go on a mission to the court of Spain.

Rubens had many secret meetings with young King Philip and his gloomy prime minister. Skillfully and earnestly he urged them to talk peace with England, and at last the King decided to ask King Charles of England to send an ambassador to Spain.

Through the long winter months Rubens waited anxiously for word that the ambassador would come. In spite of agonizing gout in his foot, he painted portraits of the royal family. The King, who was more interested in painting than in affairs of state, loved to visit Rubens' studio.

The King's court painter Velasquez came to admire the paintings of the famous Flemish artist, and Rubens praised the younger painter's brilliant portraits of the royal family.

News came at last that the English ambassador was on his way to Madrid. Rubens, believing that his mission of peace had been accomplished, hoped to return to Antwerp. But King Philip had other plans for this skillful and gracious ambassador from Flanders. So greatly did the King value Rubens' services, that he asked the Flemish painter to go as his ambassador to King Charles of England.

So in the spring of 1629 Rubens set out on a mission of peace to England, wearing a ring set with sparkling diamonds, a present from the King of Spain.

AMBROSIO SPINOLA

Courtesy of the City Art Museum, St. Louis

Rubens rode full speed over the mountains, across France, into Flanders, stopping only a few days in Antwerp in order to organize his workshop. Then one June day Rubens boarded a British warship which took him to England.

Rubens was fifty-two years old when he started on his mission to King Charles. In spite of painful attacks of gout, he looked strong and healthy and very handsome.

"He is not only clever," wrote one of King Charles' ministers, when Rubens arrived in England, "but also knows how to win the esteem of everyone and especially the King, my master."

Rubens had many long talks with the English King. Earnestly he begged King Charles to arrange a treaty with Spain. He wrote long letters to King Philip's prime minister, reporting on the progress of his talks. In July Rubens wrote that King Charles was ready to negotiate a peace. "Having carried out the order which the King our master . . . did me the honor to give me," wrote Rubens, "I beg your excellency to give me permission to return home."

While Rubens waited for another ambassador to arrive from Spain, he found time to talk with the distinguished scholars and scientists he met in London.

"Certainly in this island I find none of the crudeness which one might expect," he wrote to a friend.

On warm summer days he loved to ride through the rich green countryside. He painted pictures too.

To celebrate the peace for which he had worked so hard, he painted a beautiful landscape picture for the King, showing Saint George delivering Saint Agnes from the dragon. Saint George, who looked like King Charles, was clad in shining armor, one foot resting on the dragon's head. Gallantly he offered his arm to the beautiful Saint Agnes, who had the features of Queen Henrietta Maria. In the background, on the banks of the winding river Thames stood King Charles' turreted castle. The kneeling women and children in the forground were giving thanks to the saint who had delivered them from the terrible dragon. Two cupids descended in a bright ray from heaven, bearing crowns of laurel for the King and Queen.

SAINT GEORGE IN LANDSCAPE

Buckingham Palace, London

Winter came and still the ambassador from Spain had not arrived.

"I should like to return home and remain there all my life," Rubens wrote to a friend.

But while he waited, he continued to paint pictures for King Charles. The King, hoping to rival his mother-in-law, Marie de' Medici, asked Rubens to decorate the ceiling of his banquet hall with paintings glorifying the reign of his father, James I.

Before the Spanish ambassador arrived, Rubens had made nine glowing oil sketches for the royal dining room. Large paintings were made from these sketches after Rubens returned to Antwerp.

One sketch showed King James' baby son, Prince Charles, being crowned by two goddesses who represented England and Scotland. In this way Rubens showed that James I had united the two countries under one crown.

England and Scotland in red and yellow draperies held a golden crown over the prince's head, while Britania, a helmeted goddess in violet draperies, held the crown in place. Two cupids floated above the child bearing the royal coat of arms. Below, another cupid set fire to a pile of armor which was no longer needed because the war between the two countries had ended.

Early in the winter of 1630 the Spanish ambassador arrived, and the King held a glittering reception for him at his court. When the elaborate celebrations were over, Rubens planned to return to Antwerp, but the new ambassador needed Rubens' help and begged him to remain in England a little longer.

One day in March King Charles honored Rubens by making him a knight at a special ceremony in the royal palace. The Flemish painter knelt before the King who struck him on the shoulder with a jewel-handled sword. Before Rubens left, Charles presented him with the sword, a diamond ring and a hat-band set with sparkling jewels.

A few days later Sir Peter Paul Rubens set sail for Antwerp.

ENGLAND AND SCOTLAND CROWNING CHARLES
(Sketch for Whitehall ceiling)

The Minneapolis Institute of Art, Minneapolis

Rubens was overjoyed to be in his home again, with his two tall handsome sons. Albert was now a young man of sixteen, "seriously engaged in the study of antiquities," Rubens wrote to a friend.

Rubens' friends welcomed him warmly and were eager to entertain him. He was invited often to the home of Daniel Fourment, a rich silk merchant who had eleven beautiful daughters. Rubens loved the gay happy family and was especially charmed by Daniel's youngest daughter, the startingly pretty Helena. Sixteen-year-old Helena was flattered that this famous artist and diplomat who had been honored by Kings and princes in many countries, seemed to be attracted by her beauty. Although Rubens was fifty-three years old, he was still handsome, and his gallant manners delighted young Helena.

Suddenly Rubens realized that he was very much in love, and one day he told Daniel Fourment that he wanted to marry his youngest daughter.

Helena and Rubens were married in a big church in Antwerp, one December day in 1630. Rubens was almost dazzled by the fresh blond beauty of his young bride. Gay Helena was delighted with the balls and banquets which were given in honor of the newly married couple.

When the celebrations were over Helena and Peter Paul settled in Rubens' fine Antwerp home. Albert and Nicholas welcomed their pretty stepmother who brought laughter and gayety to their big house.

Rubens started to paint again with enthusiasm. Helena posed for him wearing her richly embroidered wedding gown, and again in a black velvet street dress. Rubens painted nineteen portraits of his beautiful wife, and the paintings glowed with light and color.

One lovely picture showed Rubens leading his wife into his home. Rubens was dressed in black, and Helena wore a yellow and black gown and a big, straw hat trimmed with tulips. Behind them walked twelve-year-old Nicholas dressed in a suit of red velvet. In the background was a gate leading into a garden filled with roses and tulips. In the foreground an old servant was feeding two brightly colored peacocks.

PROMENADE IN GARDEN

Alte Pinakothek, Munich

"At present as you have heard, I find myself by the Grace of God, beside my wife and children, at rest and with no other ambition in the world than that of living at peace," wrote Rubens happily to a friend.

Rubens' exhausting years of travel were over at last. He started once more to work on sketches illustrating the life of Henry IV, for Marie de' Medici was waiting impatiently to see the finished paintings. The biggest picture would show the King entering triumphantly into Paris. Rubens sketched the scene in pale tones against a brownish background. Henry, dressed in armor, rode in a golden chariot drawn by white horses. Above floated the goddess of victory holding a laurel wreath over the King's head. The helmeted goddess of war was driving the chariot, and Apollo followed with his lyre. Surrounding the chariot as it moved toward a triumphal arch were men carrying banners and torches and musicians playing their instruments. Behind walked prisoners of war, while in the foreground groups of men, women and children were watching the procession.

Assistants were starting to make a painting from Rubens' sketch, when suddenly the work was interrupted. From France came news that Marie de' Medici had been banished from her palace. Cardinal Richelieu, powerful prime minister of France, fearing the Queen Mother's influence over her son, persuaded King Louis to send his mother into exile. A few months later, Marie de' Medici sent word to the Archduchesse that she was on her way to Flanders.

The Queen called at Rubens' home and admired his beautiful collection of art treasures. She begged Rubens to help her in her fight to overthrow the hated Richelieu. Rubens, shocked that Marie de' Medici had been banished by her son, agreed to ask the King of Spain to send money and soldiers to aid the Queen.

"The Queen has told me," Rubens wrote to the Spanish prime minister, "that she will never come to an agreement with the King, her son, while the cardinal remains on earth."

"I have never worked for war," Rubens continued, but he added, "it will be necessary to send some assistance promptly."

TRIUMPHAL ENTRY OF HENRY IV

Metropolitan Museum of Art, New York City

In vain Rubens begged the King of Spain to send help to the banished French Queen. Marie de' Medici never returned to France, and the paintings glorifying the life of her husband were never finished. Rubens put away the magnificent oil sketches which he had made for the French Queen and started to work on a big altarpiece which the Archduchesse had ordered for a church in Brussels.

The central panel told the story of how the Spanish bishop, Saint Ildefonso, came into his church early one morning and saw the Virgin sitting before the altar, surrounded by a group of saints. As the bishop threw himself on his knees before the Virgin's throne, the Madonna held out to him a priest's robe which she had embroidered with her own hands.

Rubens painted a beautiful dark-haired Madonna dressed in a red robe and blue cloak. In the golden light, which shined on her from above, floated three cupids holding a wreath of flowers. Four fair-haired women saints who looked like the lovely Helena stood on the steps beside the Virgin. Saint Ildefonso was dressed in robes of white and scarlet. In the side panels of the altarpiece, Rubens painted portraits of the Archduchesse and her husband. Behind the kneeling Albert stood a bearded saint wearing the scarlet robes of a cardinal, while behind the Archduchesse stood a saint wearing nun's robes.

This glowing altarpiece was Rubens' last tribute to his friend the Archduchesse whom he had served so long and well. Soon after the painting was finished, Archduchesse Isabella, governor of Flanders, died. Rubens felt the loss deeply, for he loved and respected the kind ruler who, like Rubens, had worked for peace in Europe.

"Our princess shows neither great love, nor great hate; she is sweet and kind to all," Rubens once wrote about the Archduchesse.

From Spain came word that King Philip had appointed his brother, young Prince-Cardinal Ferdinand, to be the new ruler of Flanders. So early in the winter of 1635 the city governors of Antwerp asked Rubens to design street decorations to celebrate the arrival.

ST. ILDEFONSO ALTARPIECE

Kunsthistoricshes Museum, Vienna

"Today I am so overburdened with the preparations for the triumphal entry of the Prince-Cardinal that I have time neither to live nor write," Rubens wrote to a friend.

In a few weeks Rubens designed lavish decorations for the Antwerp streets, while in his workshop assistants were busily carrying out Rubens' designs for elaborate arches and an ornate triumphal car. The gout in his foot gave him such pain that he often had to be pushed about his workshop in a wheel chair.

One warm April day, guns boomed and trumpets blared as Prince-Cardinal Ferdinand rode into Antwerp. As he passed through the city gate, a carriage shaped like a ship, filled with beautiful girls dressed like goddesses, rode to meet him. On a pedestal in the center of the wagon stood a tower of spears, armor and banners. Bound prisoners of war knelt at the foot of the pedestal. As the triumphal car stopped before the Prince-Cardinal, one of the lovely girls who represented Antwerp offered him a laurel wreath on a golden plate.

On toward the center of town rode Ferdinand, passing under a row of ornate triumphal arches. On a magnificently decorated stage in front of the Town Hall, the city governors waited to receive their new ruler.

When the welcoming speeches were over, Ferdinand asked if he might meet the famous artist who had designed the brilliant decorations in his honor. But Rubens, tortured by an agonizing attack of gout, was unable to leave his home.

The next day a royal coach drove into the courtyard of the Rubens' home. Excitedly Helena rushed to tell her husband that Prince-Cardinal Ferdinand had come to congratulate Rubens on the grandeur of his work.

Ferdinand admired Rubens' art collection and inspected the busy workshop. He visited the artist's studio which was filled with glowing oil sketches, and he was charmed by the lovely Helena.

Before he left, he offered Rubens a big salary and invited him to become his court painter.

TRIUMPHAL CAR

Antwerp Museum, Antwerp

Helena's first child was born two years after she and Peter Paul were married. They named the baby girl Clara-Joanna in memory of little Clara-Serena who had died nine years before. One year later Frans Rubens was born. When Helena's second girl was born the following year, she named her Isabella-Helena.

Although the Rubens workshop was as busy as ever, Peter Paul spent many happy hours with his family, for, since the death of the Archduchesse, he seldom visited the court in Brussels. He found time to write long letters to his many friends, discussing books he had read or art treasures he had collected. In the spring he used to take long rides out into the country.

One warm summer day, soon after Isabella-Helena was born, Rubens invited his wife to drive to the country with him. Helena chatted happily as they drove through peaceful green farmland. After a few hours the carriage turned into a small road lined with trees. Through the trees Helena could see fat sheep grazing in the fields and, in the distance, the pointed roofs of a big farm. The carriage rumbled across a wooden bridge, past a little lake and a shady orchard. Then suddenly Helena saw through an opening in the trees a magnificent stone castle surrounded by a moat of water. This splendid turreted mansion, Peter Paul explained, would be their summer home. He had bought the spacious castle, the farm, the lake and the shady orchard as a present for his lovely wife. Helena was overjoyed.

All through the warm summer months Rubens, Helena and the children lived in the castle of stone, or castle of Steen as Rubens named it. They received visitors cordially. Gay Helena loved the big parties which Peter Paul planned for his many guests.

Rubens was glad to be far from the noise and bustle of Antwerp. He painted happy pictures of his wife and children, and radiant canvases showing elegant lords and ladies walking and embracing in a vast wooded park. In many of the pictures the gray stone towers of Steen could be seen in the distance.

PARK OF CASTLE OF STEEN

Kunsthistorisches Museum, Vienna

Rubens never tired of painting his beautiful young wife. In some pictures, blonde, radiant-skinned Helena was a court lady dressed in silks and satins, in some a Christian martyr, and in others a beautiful Greek goddess.

He loved to paint her as a wife and mother. In some pictures her blonde hair was brushed away from her ears and fell in ringlets down her neck. In other portraits it was combed in bangs and flowed loosely over her shoulders. In one picture a small black beret with a white plume covered her blonde head.

Rubens painted Helena waiting for her carriage on the steps of her Antwerp home. She was arrayed in a rich gown of black satin. Behind her stood a young page dressed in red. Once Rubens painted Helena as she was coming from her bath, wrapped in a dark, fur-lined cloak.

Peter Paul painted Helena with her children. Little Frans, wearing only a black beret decorated with a white plume, sat timidly on his mother's knee.

Frans was three years old when his father painted him again, sitting on his mother's lap, dressed in a silk suit and the same black beret. In one hand he held a bird's perch and in the other a string attached to a bird which fluttered in the background. Little Clara-Joanna, wearing a big starched cap, stood beside her mother. Helena wore a simple, light blue gown. Her face was shaded by a big, gray felt hat with a sweeping plume.

Although Rubens never finished this canvas, and the background of pillars and draperies is roughly painted in tones of golden brown, the figures of Helena and her two oldest children are full of life and vigor. The picture is one of the most charming family portraits that Rubens ever painted.

HELENA FOURMENT WITH HER CHILDREN

Louvre, Paris

Rubens continued to paint pictures for Kings and princes, but he no longer had to serve as an ambassador to their courts.

"Now by the divine Grace I have found peace of mind," he wrote to a friend, "having renounced every sort of employment outside my beloved profession."

When the paintings for King Charles' banquet hall were ready to send to England, Sir Peter Paul sent word to the King that he was sending an assistant who would supervise the hanging of the pictures.

"Inasmuch as I have a horror of courts," he wrote "I sent my work to England in the hands of someone else."

King Charles was delighted with Rubens' ceiling paintings glorifying his father's reign; but the extravagant King was penniless and could not pay the artist what he owed him. Three years went by before King Charles sent Rubens the promised money and a special gift of a heavy gold chain to wear around his neck.

"I should have gone there in person," wrote Rubens while he was waiting for the King to pay him; but so content was Peter Paul in his happy home that he was determined to avoid "every disturbance and intrigue."

In the peaceful country of Steen he painted pictures for his own enjoyment, lively paintings which glowed with warmth and color. One picture showed a group of barefoot men and women dancing out-of-doors. The women were wearing simple Flemish dress, while the men were dressed in the style of Italian shepherds. Hands joined, the peasants were swinging into a spirited dance. Some of the couples were holding up their handkerchiefs to form a bridge for the other couples to run under. Sitting in a tree above the dancing couples was a peasant who accompanied the dancers on a flute. On the right a charming Italian villa could be seen in the distance, while on the left stretched a shadowy Flemish landscape of green trees and rolling hills.

PEASANT DANCE

Prado, Madrid

Over and over the woods and fields, the winding streams and wide skies of Steen appeared in Rubens' paintings. Sometimes his turreted stone castle made a background for his pictures, and in other paintings the pointed roof tops of his farm houses could be seen in the distance.

He painted the rich countryside in every kind of light—as it appeared in the gray light of early morning, by moonlight, or at sunset when peasants were returning from their work. The effect of changing lights on color fascinated him, and his brilliant canvases shone with a new radiance. For the first time Rubens realized that a landscape could make a picture in itself. He loved to paint the fresh countryside after a heavy rain when sunlight filtered through a cloudy sky, picking out bright patches on the trees and fields.

He painted a radiant scene just after a sudden storm. In the foreground a farmer was driving home his cattle. Some of the cows were stopping to drink in a stream beside the road. Another farmer was walking down the road between two milkmaids. In the patch of sunlight on the left, peasants were piling hay into tall stacks.

Arching across the vast cloudy sky was a glorious double rainbow.

RAINBOW LANDSCAPE

Permission of the Wallace Collection, London

Little Peter Paul Rubens was born one day in 1637. His father was fifty-nine years old.

Rubens' handsome face had grown heavier, and he limped badly. He hardly ever left his quiet country home, but sometimes he felt strong enough to visit his Antwerp studio. Loyal Frans Snyders was still in charge of Rubens' busy workshop, but young Anthony Van Dyke had gone to England, and was painting brilliant portraits of King Charles and his family.

One day the Rubens workshop received an order from an Italian Duke for a painting telling of the horrors of war. Rubens, who had worked so hard for peace, knew exactly how he would illustrate this subject. With amazing speed he painted the picture and sent it off to Italy.

"Please God you may receive it soon," he wrote to the Duke's reresentative in Italy. "Concerning the subject of the picture," Rubens continued, "... I will explain it in a few words."

Venus, goddess of love, Rubens wrote, was clinging to the armored god, Mars, who was rushing off to war; while an angry goddess symbolizing fury was pulling Mars on to destruction. Falling in confusion under the feet of the advancing war gods were men and women who represented the good and beautiful things which war destroys. A man holding an architect's tool represented buildings, a woman with a broken lute was supposed to be harmony and a mother holding a crying child symbolized the family.

"That lugubrious matron, clad in black and with her veil torn..." wrote Rubens, "is unhappy Europe, afflicted for so many years by plunder, outrage and misery."

"I am by nature and inclination a peaceful man," Rubens wrote to a friend. Tirelessly he had worked to keep the peace in Europe, and now once again in this forceful painting, Rubens had served the cause of peace.

THE HORRORS OF WAR

Pitti Gallery, Florence

Photo Alinari

"I am sorry not to be the able man that his Eminence once knew," wrote sixty-two-year-old Rubens to a cardinal who commissioned him to paint a picture. Politely he asked the cardinal to excuse him from the work. His right hand often pained him so terribly that sometimes he could not hold a brush. Because he could no longer work on the paintings he had designed for King Philip's hunting lodge, he urged his assistants to sign their own names to the finished pictures.

One day when he was feeling stronger, Rubens painted a portrait of himself dressed in a black cloak lined with velvet. His left hand rested on the hilt of his sword. A glove covered his crippled right hand which held a cane. His face which was framed by a white ruff and broad-brimmed black hat was still handsome, but his heavy, sad eyes told a story of great suffering.

He hardly ever spoke of the agonizing pain which attacked him more and more often. In his letters to his friends he discussed the works of other artists and the pictures he planned to paint. When one of his favorite pupils was married in the spring of 1640, Rubens rejoiced with him in his happiness. "I and my wife . . . wish you and your beloved with all our hearts great happiness and perfect lasting contentedness in your station."

This was the last letter Rubens was able to write for a few days later his hands were completely paralyzed. Helena called in Antwerp's best doctors, but they could not help her husband. From Brussels came word that Prince-Cardinal Ferdinand was sending two of Flanders most skilled doctors to tend the famous artist. While Helena waited for the doctors to arrive she hardly ever left her husband's bedside. Then, early one morning before the doctors reached the Rubens' home, Peter Paul Rubens died. He was sixty-three years old.

Three days later a majestic funeral took place in the church of St. Jacques in Antwerp. Dukes and princes, bishops and cardinals, and many of Europe's most noted artists and scholars came to pay their last tribute to a great artist who had lived a rich and noble life.

"It is not how long one lives," Rubens once wrote to a friend, "but how well."

SELF PORTRAIT

Kunsthistorisches Museum, Vienna

BIBLIOGRAPHY

Bertram, Anthony: *The Life of Sir Peter Paul Rubens.* Peter Davies Ltd., London, 1928.

Burckhardt, Jacob: *Recollections of Rubens.* Phaidon Press Ltd., London, 1950.

Cammaerts, Emile: *Rubens Painter and Diplomat.* Faber and Faber Ltd., London, 1932.

Dillon, Edward: *Rubens.* Methuen and Co., London, 1909.

Fry, Roger: *French, Flemish and British Art.* Coward McCann Inc., New York, 1951.

Goris, Jan Albert and Held, S. Julius: *Rubens in America.* Pantheon Books Inc., New York, 1947.

Harsanyi, Zosoltde: *The Lover of Life.* Translated from the Hungarian by Paul Tabor in collaboration with Willa and Edwin Muir. G. P. Putnam's Sons, New York, 1942.

Larsen, Erik: *Peter Paul Rubens.* De Sikkel, Antwerp, 1952.

Magurn, Ruth Saunders: *The Letters of Peter Paul Rubens.* Translated and edited by Ruth Saunders Magurn. Harvard University Press, Cambridge, 1955.

Michel, Emile: *Rubens, His Life, His Works and His Time.* Translated by Elizabeth Lee. Charles Scribner's Sons, New York, 1899.

Peter Paul Rubens. Librairie Hachette, Paris.

Rooses, Max: *L'Oeuvre de Peter Paul Rubens.* Jos. Maes, Editeurs, Anvers, 1886.

Rubens Paintings and Drawings. Phaidon edition. Oxford University Press, New York, 1939.

Terrasse, Charles: *Rubens.* Librairie Renouard, Paris, 1935.

Wallack, Ira: *The Horn and the Roses.* Boni and Baer, New York, 1947.